"Delectable, magical, and sparkly tomorrows: these words glittered in my brain as I devoured pimentel mendoza's *MY BOYFRIEND APOCALYPSE*. A mixture of eroticism, queer yearning, and transformative grief—antmen pimentel mendoza asks us to imagine and materialize what a future-oriented and world-making apocalypse looks like. Whether it is the way our 'flesh betrays our secret stinks' or 'if a starry sky waits on the other side,' pimentel mendoza reminds us how being ravaged and unraveled can feel oh-so-gratifying, opening us to new dimensions of pleasure, possibility, and existence we have not thought of before."

MT VALLARTA
author of *What You Refuse to Remember*

"In *MY BOYFRIEND APOCALYPSE*, antmen pimentel mendoza offers us language for survival in a world on fire: with intimacy, humor, and precision. pimentel mendoza deftly weaves together pop music with queer confessional, diasporic memory with digital ephemera, crafting a lush lyric that delights and devastates. Reading these poems feels like scrolling through a well-curated library of screenshots from a friend who understands you better than you might understand yourself: witty, vulnerable, and unforgettably poignant. *MY BOYFRIEND APOCALYPSE* is a sharp, memorable debut."

LAUREL CHEN

"For those of us still coming to terms with global health crises and general sense of everything being a total trash fire, antmen pimentel mendoza's *MY BOYFRIEND APOCALYPSE* is the antidote to doomscrolling our way to numbness. Drawing on internet trends, pop music references, post-therapy assessments, and more, pimentel mendoza skillfully makes a case for seemingly mundane acts like ass eating as a political gesture in a book that insists 'Spill, baby' and cheekily (tenderly) asks you 'to fold / your way / into more bravery, or at least, fewer fonts of shame.' This book seems to recognize no bounds to radical love, sex, and survival in a time when we keep waking up to the chill world ending. In the face of incessant apocalypse, pimentel mendoza beckons us to laugh, fuck, fall in love, and hold each other for just a minute longer."

MURIEL LEUNG
author of *Imagine Us* and *The Swarm*

NOMADIC PRESS

OAKLAND

PHILADELPHIA

XALAPA

WWW.NOMADICPRESS.ORG

MASTHEAD

FOUNDING PUBLISHER
J. K. Fowler

LEAD EDITOR
Maw Shein Win

ASSOCIATE EDITOR
Michaela Mullin

DESIGN
Jevohn Tyler Newsome

MISSON STATEMENT Through publications, events, and active community participation, Nomadic Press collectively weaves together platforms for intentionally marginalized voices to take their rightful place within the world of the written and spoken word. Through our limited means, we are simply attempting to help right the centuries' old violence and silencing that should never have occurred in the first place and build alliances and community partnerships with others who share a collective vision for a future far better than today.

INVITATIONS Nomadic Press wholeheartedly accepts invitations to read your work during our open reading period every year. To learn more or to extend an invitation, please visit: www.nomadicpress.org/invitations

DISTRIBUTION
Orders by teachers, libraries, trade bookstores, or wholesalers:

Nomadic Press Distribution
orders@nomadicpress.org
(510) 500-5162

Small Press Distribution
spd@spdbooks.org
(510) 524-1668 / (800) 869-7553

This book was made possible by a loving community of chosen family and friends, old and new. For author questions or to book a reading at your bookstore, university/school, or alternative establishment, please send an email to info@nomadicpress.org.

Cover art and author portrait by Arthur Johnstone

Published by Nomadic Press, 1941 Jackson Street, Suite 20, Oakland, CA 94612
First printing, 2023

Library of Congress Cataloging-in-Publication Data

Title: *MY BOYFRIEND APOCALYPSE*
p. cm.
Summary: With a disco ball as a north star, *MY BOYFRIEND APOCALYPSE* responds to the myriad, simultaneous apocalypses we are and are not surviving, from the everyday crises of being a body to the global emergencies of devastating climate change and unfettered white supremacy. These poems ask what it would be like to make out with the end of the world: Who slipped tongue first? Is the apocalypse a good kisser? Are you?

[1. **POETRY** / American / Asian American & Pacific Islander. 2. **POETRY** / LGBTQ+. 3. **POETRY** / American / General.]

LIBRARY OF CONGRESS CONTROL NUMBER: 2022947224
ISBN: 978-1-955239-38-7

MY BOYFRIEND APOCALYPSE

9/2023

Roregan—
Thank you for
your support!

MY BOYFRIEND
APOCALYPSE

antmen pimentel mendoza

**NOMADIC
PRESS**

Oakland · Philadelphia · Xalapa

CONTENTS

introduction

INTRODUCTION

*The storm irresistibly propels him into the future to
which his back is turned, while the pile of debris before
him grows skyward. This storm is what we call progress.*

Walter Benjamin, trans. Harry Zohn

*If you feel it let it happen
Keep on dancin' till the world ends*

Britney Spears

Though I wrote the earliest drafts of some of these poems in the
preceding summer, the project did not take its shape until the ways
my work, my art, and my thoughts are organized and contained were
rendered vital and life-sustaining—as if for the first time—in the
spring of 2020. That March, the world was ending.

But isn't the end of the world tediously ordinary? And on the
utterly regular occasion of the world ending, shouldn't I let my dreams
be the organizing principle for the world I am building with you to
take its place?

When I say apocalypse is ordinary I mean that worlds end all
the time. As a teenager, my high school boyfriend found a new love
and my world ended. At twenty-five, my nanay passed and my world
ended. I mean this, too, on another scale: when a certain voracious
European sailed his ocean blue, the world ended. With the violent
legislative and Supreme Court efforts to reverse what small gains in

bodily autonomy the oppressed have won in this (world-endingly) disastrous experiment of statehood on stolen land, the world ends. Worlds end with bullets, at knife points, in a housing crisis, on military bases, in the carceral state. They end, and still here we are.

And still here I was: Listening to pop music, organizing the poems into this project, watching 90 Day Fiancé, ordering delivery, and masking up for the grocery store. I teetered dangerously closely to despair. I fell again and again into bouts of hopelessness, but then I would go to bed. I would wake in the morning, put on the same soft clothes, and hop onto the first of many Zoom calls. Even as I teetered, I was also held. I was held by beloved community, by practice, by abolitionist Miriam Kaba's reminder that "hope is a discipline."

It was in this tenuous balance between the dark and the discipline that I decided to fall in love. I was in love with my then-partner, I was in love with my life (and I love living it), but why not fall in love with this (apparently inevitable) end of the world itself? In a dormitory in Tacoma, Washington, I told my friend Dallas that I think of poetry, like queerness, as an orientation to the world, a willingness to fall in love with anything enough to take it to the page and spend some of my precious time with it. If I am to live through this apocalypse—and the next one and the one after that—then let me take him to the page, spend some time with him, and fall in love.

This is *MY BOYFRIEND APOCALYPSE*. I mean apocalypse is my boyfriend and we do make out. I mean the end of the world is an apocalypse and all my boyfriends past and present are trying their best to survive it, too. I mean to write towards the small corner of apocalypse that is mine and mine only and it's personal except it's yours now, too. We've survived and I'm so glad. We're surviving and I love that for us.

HOME ALONE AFTER THERAPY, THE AUTHOR CONSIDERS A HOUSEPLANT

                             Baby,   dance
your tangelo blooms under that verdant candelabra
with your flat feet slapping off the laminate planet
and the cotton briefs scarce on your yes-yes area

with nothing else to bear. Baby,   Kelis sings
she's got your money, and yes, the shake-thrust
of your hips is an inch-wide swish toward a future
after capital. Baby,   stretch

before you reach your hands for the stem and leaf
refrains, those reminders to breathe. Baby,   these giants
you laugh under are you, too. Baby,   velvet
your palms with almond oils and bump bellies,

the gods decree you share your gold. Baby,   remember,
too, the sea and loss, the reason tucked behind habits
in your wallet, pressed against a photo of Nanay.
Baby,   feed yourself, say thank you, write home.

                  Spill,   baby.

ON GRAMMAR

a grammar of my syrup:

the varying coarsenesses of pubic hair,
armpit hair, well-manicured beard hair,
neglected beard hair, bushy eyebrows

a grammar incompatible with sense:

discipline or a place where Toni Collette
and arithmetic meet and she has that accent
I forget every time or a jelly spilling out
papel picado stinger-streamers singing
anthemic disco tunes about the romances
of the dead and unengaged or uninspired

a grammar of facing:

the bright laminate of a bedroom floor
flexing under the weight of one foot
cum slipper then another and all then

a grammar (room for sunlight):

the cruelty of learning to forgive
every year just as she makes her
early exits—a small joy, and
everything—she can fall where she
likes and I am not compelled to turn
long pig on a spit with all the fixin's

MY BOYFRIEND, THE APOCALYPSE

1932

THE POET'S FUNCTION

THE POET   the future   the depressing notion
the irreparable divorce   the
magnificent fruit

                                        will assume
                                                    and
                        press upon   the depth
of   each other
                    human   destruction
                    would instantaneously   null and
void   objective   realities and
                        virtue   one
hand

        readily slips into the

                                        god. The poet

of   phenomenon
of intuitive

                                        produce
          will put an end to

                                        men
          all men, renounce
order
          We shall   cry   each time
more or less
                                        subject to
                              existence
          we manage   a lovely, lasting
                                        mingling with
the light of day, and will not have
greater   intimacy

GHAZAL FOR THE END OF THE WORD

Once we leave this language behind, we'll speak to each other
in dream-pictures and maps: all we've survived 'til each other.

I'll abandon these limbs, be something more serpentine. Earth
bellied, leather egged, and quick-tongued: still we'll know each other.

Fact: I know the spikes in blood sugar make me enjoy cookies
a whole lot less. Hope to stay within your warm reach, mother.

I have a Word doc I've saved under the file name "Thirty
by Thirty." *Make peace with my body*, we promise each other.

The lizard-baby in me says *Lighttthh! Cameraths! Acttthhun!*
He means fight or flight, keep the show going for each other.

Maybe our flesh betrays our secret stinks, a perverse folk
legend the same yellow way birds warble with each other.

Auntie asks me, *Are we the same kind of brown?* and I hear
Did we take the same route here? That's how we hold each other.

AUBADE WHEN A MORNING
LASTS DAYS

Because there has been no   leaving
          for   months,

and the next   night will be a pink lady
apple.   Because we spent our last   night

as   a bruising   s   kin forgetting-
forgotten though you and I would not afford

to void,   could not afford
not to retain.   You and I   a cauldron

god's thumb   printed on our island
lake.   Impossible shaped mourn-

ing,   endless opal mourning for the
hotplates I tell you   might be

afritada or   kaldereta   or   mechado.
Let's take up a new shape: the salted

vertices where   hands   take measure
How long   can we h   old

our   breath   if a starry sky waits
on the other side?   I say mourn-

ing because we remain   incalculably
quilted, staunchly   northern, deliberately

exposed. I say   mourning because
a tether   cannot jeweltone   her way

into habitat.   Because a season
of mornings   reflects   too.

THE TAKOYAKI VENDING MACHINES AND I

I think of Agnès' Glaneurs when my pinky toenail blushes
up on six foot radials queued outside the Gilman Whole Foods;
which is to say nothing can feel this essential all of the time. Bare

vines sprouting arterial from the umbilical phantom, motherlink,
or chili cheese dog of an I-580 embankment stare Joel
in his underbelly eye, recites his usual brunch order. I void

and watch wordless GoPro videos on YouTube of first
person taste testing Japanese and Singaporean
vending machine-made meals like udon and burgers.

(A soundtrack: coins in the palm, cellophane vessel pregnant
with steam, cardboard pull tab orchestra.) I void and massage
my century egg eyes scrambled white easy or mooncake

doughy. When I take my therapy appointment
on Zoom, I don't ride the 6; which is to say I do not have to think
of Telegraph's gleaners, adjacent Walgreens and Taste

of Denmark. Voided now, I dream the coquette oaks and pines
my friend shoots on his midday hike and tide away the cyberpunk cafe
where only my hands remember counting days or howling in the night.

QUARANTINE PARADE OF ROSES

My favorite kind of touch stretches me into the future,
pulls me more accommodating. Here: bells for food,

bells for a ride on your bullet train, bells for you to hold
me and render. In a lineup of bare bums, a pink blooms

in the vase-mouth of mine. My favorite touch is miasmic,
a laugh settling into my hand on the hairs of your forearm.

A lesson blood teaches me: there is such a thing as too-sweet.
My favorite touch points to prosody, asks macabre shapes

of my mouth, invites tongues to consider ugly and intrepid.
Do mosquitoes like diabetic blood? I wonder in Mexico City,

counting goose-pimpled mounds and dimples on my love's
skin against those on mine.

A LOSING DOG BREATHES INTO WARRIOR II

The wick burns eucalyptus tempered wax quick / until we spare

mercy, birth-blow soot phantoms / incensed smoke taking shape

as my body bent over / ass facing north. I strike again and moan

to crack and spark along to a song, probably asking you to fold

your way / into more bravery or, at least, fewer fonts of shame.

That den fills thick with fragrance, calling you / "baby boy"

and "sweets" in Johnnie Walker soda tones / but on a yoga mat, too,

I swear, I'm good for you / Tell me no, tell me no, someone please.

I LEAN INTO THE THROAT OF SUMMER

hung vine lovely boy with arm muscles :: popsicle
syrup drip, pore strip, and semi-permanent ash hair dye

pedal, pedal, whiz :: a backyard temple combination plate
and a probiotic aperitif

leg silk on leg silk and late summer harvest heft of sugarsweet
fruit in my hand, in my mouth :: my mouth open in May

> I kiss you, the meridian of you, running long from the heavy
> > custard
> apples. I kiss and know the ends of you, know the makings of you.

fielding, visions, pointing, floats :: with eyes closed I see an imagined
end, the neon fluff swimming just beyond what I can know

> Later, I trace my own seam with my foot up on the tiled shower
> > wall.

MY BOYFRIEND
APOCALYPSE

I cried oral reef ugly today.
In the hospital bed,

day three: Destiny's Child rises
again and it's not that

I think Beyoncé is above
critique, but I never

look the light of day in the mouth.
Dog breath mornings, I say.

Strings of popcorn worn like pearls,
an underwater lake for bones,

whatever gets us through today's
apocalypse, I say.

I have my optimist hat on
today. "No one's happy,"

I write and it's the truth but feels
uncouth. I'll explain to 'Tay

I think we can make it happen,
that no one's happy the way I am

to hear he is learning rest.
Who cradles us? Just this

side of teenage, half-creased
by cheap whiskey, doubled

in mass of moth wings. Who cares
for our tomorrows? Why—outside

a bar, outside a series of bars
you might call a pattern—

who calls for us? Who has the rights
to visit? Uses them?

MY GOLDEN RECORD
MELTED INTO INGOTS

AFTER PAIGE LEWIS & TORRIN A. GREATHOUSE

We preoccupy ourselves with justice then refuse to do it. Here are two ways our bodies can look. And here are two bodies we find repulsive. Unbind them to learn two is not enough. Once I watched the same six second video of a child pointing at a gaggle of geese and demanding, "Look at all those chickens" on repeat until I called everyone I know by a better name. These are two ways a body can look. Point your finger on the parts that set fires. Do you have fingers? Two is not enough. We care if the ones who die are familiar to us. We throw leather around and find joy in it. This is a record—this is music—this is a grooved disc of wax—this is a way to tell more than two. Some of us are allowed to kill. Some of us are able to eat because of how we kill. Eating is everything we do to sustain our physical bodies. (Here are two ways our bodies can look). We eat plants and we eat animals. Animal is the name we give to the beasts whose speech we cannot learn. Learning is what we call our thirst for you. Two is not enough. From here, we measure greatness against the ability to fathom. Like for enjoyment, I might plant a seed, might watch something with wings from my window. "Engineer" is the word we use to celebrate the death of greatness. For example, some men sorted seeds and called some "mine" or some men built winged vessels. Do you find us grotesque? Are we too warm for you? Sometimes our heat is shocking, we know. When you find us, will you unburden us from ourselves?

Will you look at our ribs and see a chart of future endeavors? Will you watch us comb our hair and know the reason for rain? Will you save us from history, boil us into shiny machines, animal fat processors, keystroke keepers, ox horn milk cartons, glass vase shadows?

//

We   refuse
                          our
              bodies
                    enough

        geese
                                              know
    a better name. These are   ways
              your finger   parts   fires. Do
you have   enough
              familiar   leather
        and   joy in   this
                    wax

                    to

        eat

                              something

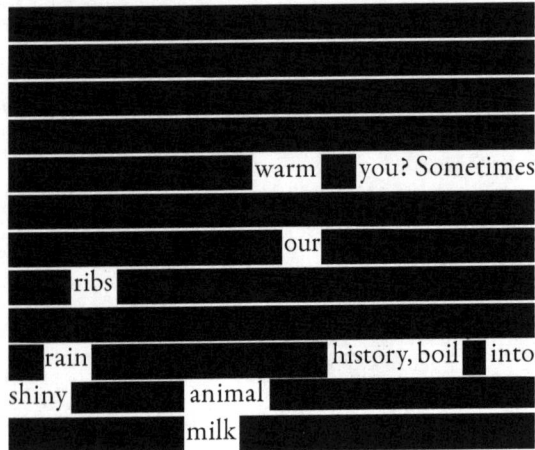

warm you? Sometimes

our

ribs

rain   history, boil   into

shiny   animal

milk

//

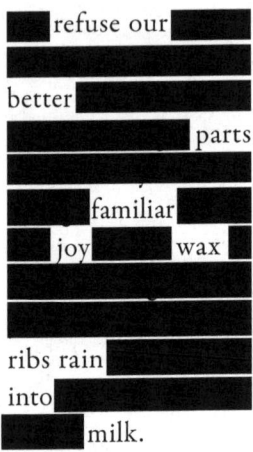

refuse our

better

parts

familiar

joy   wax

ribs rain

into

milk.

JHENÉ AIKO (THE POET) READS JOSÉ ESTEBAN MUÑOZ AND EATS A PLUOT IN A BATHHOUSE

Last night, my boyfriend asks why I taste so sweet
and I tell him that's just how I am and he goes,

"No, I mean you taste like sugar" and I go
"Oh, I just chugged some Squirt."

After my shower this morning, he bends me over,
asks me why I taste so sweet and I tell him,

"I used the rest of the Squirt as an enema."

/ /

Eating ass really had a moment the year after we
graduated. That is, straight people finally had their
field days with their cheeks.

The R&B singer sings on about eating an imagined (presumably) male partner's "booty like groceries" or so I remembered it.

In reality, she sings about a suitor and her expectations of him: namely, that he should eat her booty like groceries. This slippage in memory may be like misremembering the broadcast of a Truman Capote interview one may or may not have seen as a swishy child. A slippage that is "as exhilarating as it is terrifying" like a half-remembered Intro to Feminist Theory lecture from college.

Maybe I project that posture (she who eats) onto her (the groceries) in a hopeful negotiation in the raunch of minoritized survival: No, do not elide me, songstress: *Yes, grant me this, songstress.*

And that's the fantasy, right? Her impossibly pretty face—gentle and small features, earnest eyes—buried in a couple of fat, hairy cheeks, impeccable nail decor and polish shining as she digs into the stone fruit, her tongue lapping around the hole: at turns and bends, he's hairy, earthy, and spicy. His is a holiday pie of an asshole.

Of course I mean to say: My gender is Jhené Aiko eating manbutt.

Six years before "Post to Be" is a hit song, my high school boyfriend bends over his reluctance and the center console of the 2003 Nissan Frontier my parents let me drive to and from school. The only clothing he has on are his cotton t-shirt (slack from joining the tennis team and shaking the baby fat he wore when we met), and a pair of crew socks (tubed necks hugging his ankles). My nose and mouth are in the cleft of his ass. Though we are both 6' tall, we are well practiced at the percussive choreography of fucking in the cab of the pickup. Eating out, though, is a new, particular perversion I request after grainy amateur videos uploaded to newfangled web 2.0 video sharing platforms. My tongue lands, wide and wet, flush against and dug into this end of him. Then I hear his refrains of ewewewewewewew and grossgrossgrossgrossgross soften with my feast.

/ /

He opens in slow shakes and pulses: first come
notes from the inside

of a laundry detergent bottle—flowers,
soap, a mother washing her teenage son's under-

things—then an eruption into a small heaven:
salty iron cream of flesh.

// /

Tomorrow I will eat vanilla soft serve in a cake cone,
rolled tortilla chips, eggs over medium—the sweet

cream chills my tongue, soothing me into a summer
soak and drip—red powder on the chips will burst

fluorescent, pucker my lips vice-tight—the
custard-thick orange runs exhale-slow from the tine

of my fork to the alien contract-pull of my throat.
All day, I think of your tongue on my ass.

ON METFORMIN HYDROCHLORIDE (OR LOVE SONG FOR CARB HEAVY SNACKS FROM MY STILL-WORKING BODY)

I eat a rice cake dipped in strawberries
and cream frosting and its texture begs
to be called "curious"—I promised

poetry would be my avenue
to delight, a near-constant striving,
but what place do I set for bad news—

> I think of these meds as a brick wall / bad news
> or / I think of what compounds / I've still got
> in me / bad news / I think of human cruelty
> / (I think about strange modifiers, / I think
> of the superfluous, / my body) / I think of an
> Impossible Whopper wrapped in lettuce / I
> think the violences / I tolerate betray that / I
> think of my hands as second / and third tongues
> / I think of the flowers / I meant to collect / I
> think of my blood / on the sticks in the box with
> / the biohazard label / I think of marine life /
> not as metaphor / but as neighboring world kin

I eat a bag of salt & pepper chips—At the marina, a cloud
of precious metals swells into an open mouth—
Sometimes that mouth is me—I eat my favorite meals

and the organs fail their richness—I would learn
to roller skate if science could hack surface tension:
Jesus-blade my way into the Pacific for a visit.

THE GAY DADS IN THE MILK AD THAT TELLS ME TO "LOVE WHAT'S REAL" CONSIDER A GAY DIVORCE

I.

I am not saying I regret having the kid—I would never say that—
what I mean to say is anything true or funny, at least. Love to love you,

brown eyes on a Sunday morning with maple syrup, a beaten egg,
a loose batter. Later that night, we send Willow up to brush her teeth,

we read her *Ferdinand* again, we don't teach her bad words: "civil war"
    or "oxymoron"
or "casualty." Watching CNN, you ask me: "How long does a volcano
    have to be dormant

before it's dead?" An hour later, I read Isherwood in bed again when you
    snake in
from the two-car garage, swallow me in a kiss with your bong ripped
    open wide

whale shark mouth. What I mean to say is I do miss a bear night
at Steamworks and I regret that on most days.

II.

After we watch a Netflix doc on the meat and dairy industry, I pick up
    soy milk
from Whole Foods but Willow doesn't like the filmy way it goes down.

Milk-mustachioed Tony Hawk and milk-mustachioed Britney Spears
on gender appropriate posters gym class locker room hallways

and the food pyramid's bready base are totally corporate scams.
    Can you believe that?
I saw a headline that claims California is in shambles

because of the demand for almond milk, but the sugar in oat milk hurts
    my tummy.
On Recon, I told you I was a sub because I keep such tight coil control

in my waking hours that the prospect of slumber-fading into you
throat-first was a liberation; that there was no molasses or preserve as
    sweet

as the release it is to be nothing before you enter me, until I sheath you.
Then you took me on our first date then another.

SELF-PORTRAIT AS THE POTATO THAT FLEW AROUND MY ROOM

My freshman roommate trudged through / his wall-to-wall lagoon of clothes nose-first, / sniff-testing pairs of boxers before class. I see him / in the piles of clothing in my room and in the laugh / of your apology: "Sorry I keep cumming onto your / pillow." Nanay would say I fall hard and often and I think of / Big Pun featuring Joe and my high school boyfriend / asking, *"I just crush a lot" isn't a Mac Miller lyric?*

I am never mum. I scream from all rooftops.

I think friends are the keepers of good deeds / you don't remember but when I fall in love, I try / to hold each sweet thing myself. / In October 2014, I post a video of Frank Ocean / performing and caption it with a birthday greeting, / what do you know *about scorpio x scorpio love, Frank?* / but, really, I don't know much about that myself. / "The truth," I tell Kris, "is that I fall in love ten / times a day walking down the street." / I hope for your clemency with my slow-sudden dawn: / every set of four walls I bring you into might embarrass me. / Be gentle on my decor and the haphazard collections, / easy on every bumbling story I tell, soft with the dishes / I'll wash in a kitchen in the apartment we don't rent yet.

NAGLADLAD

I wake into a dawn
when Ate can tell us about   justice. When I slow
to   breathe, I deduct all units,
detectives, and agents.
         In the evenings, I   pardon
my ungodly selves.   Hustisya
              para kay   ganda,
                       death to empire.

an amerikano sits in fatigues

      and clutches four coins close to the mother

            of pearl, waits for head / hands aflame, vision

      oxblooded until ganda's stardust cheeks sink

true blue / a hero readymade

To (unfurl)   into a goddessness
                         like a flag

                              big enough to mean nothing,
                              big enough to gown.

To (swell)   into a silk, an older sister
                              midnighting
                              through the filigreed gate that

might surround

                              her family home.

To (fold)   communion
                              wafer breakable.

To (feed)   the village
                              with my hellish body.

ODE TO THE MOON, THE EARTH'S ONLY SATELLITE, WITH YEARS OF COGNITIVE BEHAVIORAL THERAPY

Say recovery is to believe in &   be the one I am waiting for. Say I
leapfrog hop from one lunacy to the next,   say I make moonfaces
  from

reflections of some light, the crag-wide shadows I cast   & bend
into
magic mirror filigree geometry &,   as you know, I do howl.

Say by "some light," I do mean   "me." I do mean
to confess that I have loved as dogma,

might loving show me how to love (say in the way a hopeful
mapmaker might drag his pencil into his footfall's legend).
Say

maybe I loved in the way of pathologic myth,   say old loves
were vessel for fancy, maybe   I loved like a clumsy bloom,

that's what I knew   best to do.
Is there a people who does not revere the moon,
      anyway?

Is it sacrilege to say I am a moon? But draw   near & imagine
I am a moon, always full. Imagine I do not wane. Imagine now

a two moon sky,   imagine even three. Imagine I run out of gods
for namesakes,   imagine even the minor gods are claimed.

Imagine what we'd do to the tides,   our beams shot
through the foam, say even   deep sea is bright.

A STUDENT ASKS ME ABOUT EMPIRICAL KNOWLEDGE OF THE SELF AS A PREREQUISITE TO SELF-LOVE (AND I FUMBLE THE RESPONSE)

1.

Subject always already falls
into sea-deep powder sky. I imagine

my mouth puckers. I would burst,
likely. Subject always already arrives

here, here, here. I wouldn't check my notifications
as often (always already notified). Here I dress

in organza, here in silk, here in the tendons
swimming chewy in spicy broth

of cruelty. Across the universe
of me: a horizon, an event called mother,

called reunion. Or, kindness and reverie in concert,
tersely skinned girl or cyborg or a library

of the storied always already forgotten.
Falling there will make me always already

generous with walls of gold, soft touches through
toughest chats, and custard rich kisses on the neck.

I think my iPhone has made me better
practiced at lying about what I know.

2.

What I always already know: I am
not lonely enough to chisel, desperate
enough to turn my back.

My therapist guides me in the work
of sending presents to my brain stem
(a universe suffering sugar, men,

and a mediocre public transit system
for an empty presence and a logic game).
He says, "Breathe patience and generosity

into it" and I, imagining an artichoke's stalk
glitters from the salt I've just sprinkled, meditate
on being less shitty and mean to myself.

3.

	opportunity	excitement	optimism
health & wellness	a new water bottle from Ross	calluses on the loins of my hands	gold lamé, a delicate lace, gym shoes tied tight
lifestyle	emerald	black	berry
travel	Scooby Doo style trap door hallway; limitless	Airbnb search results for: Pasay, NAIA, Metro Manila	Chapultepec; Intramuros; the Women's Building

MY BOYFRIEND, APOCALYPSE

apocalypse is not a one time event
apocalypse of color for people of color
apocalypse is a university-wide issue
apocalypse is a fuck marathon, my to-read pile
apocalypse now or later
apocalypse sink ships
Apocalypse Now was filmed in the Philippines, in part, due to low cost
apocalypse is tax dollars at work
Apocalypto (2006, dir. Mel Gibson)
apocalypse is free
apocalypse now and then
apocalypse at work from home
apocalipstick stain on your apocalypse collar
Apocalypse Now was filmed after producers wined and dined dictator
      Ferdinand Marcos
apocalypse is a one time event
apocalypse is a rally: MY BODY MY CHOICE, FACE MASKS ARE
      FOR SHEEP
apocalypse is that time I passed out at the Yuba River
apocalypse is is is is is is
Apocalypse Now was filmed in the Philippines, in part, due to the easy
      access to U.S. military vehicles on the islands

apocalypse is not an event
apocalypse gives me the blues
apocalypse to the bones, to the teeth
apocalypse is not
apocalypse now and forever

NOTES

"My Boyfriend, The Apocalypse" is a whiteout of André Breton's "The Poet's Function" from *Les Vases Communicants* (1932), as it was reprinted in Maurice Nadeau's *The History of Surrealism* (1945), translated from the French by Richard Howard and published by Collier Books in 1967.

Part of the final line of **"A Losing Dog Breathes into Warrior II"** borrows from the lyrics of Mitski's song "Thursday Girl."

"I Lean into the Throat of Summer" borrows its title from Jenny Xie's poem "Chinatown Diptych" as published in her collection *Eye Level*.

"My Golden Record Melted into Ingots" is a burning haibun, a form invented by torrin a. greathouse. In a burning haibun, a prose poem burns by erasure into a shorter poem before burning by erasure once more into a haiku.

"Jhené Aiko (The Poet) Reads José Esteban Muñoz and Eats a Pluot in a Bathhouse" quotes the phrase "as exhilarating as it is terrifying" from the introduction to José Estaban Muñoz's *Disidentifications: Queers of Color and the Performance of Politics*.

"Nagladlad" is in memory of Jennifer Laude.

READING GUIDE

APOCALYPSE NOW AND THEN

In the introduction to this book, I wrote about apocalypse as an "utterly regular occasion." Many of the poems that followed reckoned with the idea of the end of the world and how I might make peace and even flirt with it.

- **EXERCISE**: What does the apocalypse mean to you? Make a list, starting each line with "Apocalypse is..." Surprise yourself with what you might consider to be the end of the world: Exaggerate when necessary, embrace the drama.

- **DISCUSS**: What does it take to make peace with what is bigger or even scarier than our comprehension? Is facing the end of the world easier if we're laughing? If we're turned on?

REPRESENTATIVE POEMS:

"The Takoyaki Vending Machines and I" (p. 8)
"Quarantine Parade of Roses" (p. 9)
"My Boyfriend, Apocalypse." (p. 33)

END OF THE WORLD PLAYLIST

Thanks to early exposure to hours of VH1 programming, I'm a pop culture nerd. I often write from the songs, memes, movies, and celebrities that snag my attention.

- **EXERCISE**: Write a list of your favorite memes. Write another list of songs you can't get out of your head. Another list: Celebrities that you think you'd really get along with. Next, celebrities you just really wouldn't get along with. Finally, movies and TV shows you want to live in. Pick one item off of any of these lists and write in response to the question, "Why is this the most important meme/song/celebrity/movie/TV show in the world right now?" Lie if you have to. Then answer, "Why is this the worst meme/song/celebrity/movie/TV show?" Again, lie if you have to. Finally, answer, "If I said, 'this meme/song/celebrity/movie/TV show is me,' what would that mean?" When you've answered these questions to your heart's content, go on to another item in your lists. You might surprise yourself with what truths emerge from your playing, lying, and giggling.

- **DISCUSS**: What role does art have to play in a crumbling world? What about "low" art like Real Housewives or Ava Max singles?

REPRESENTATIVE POEMS:

"My Golden Record Melted into Ingots" (p. 14)
"The Gay Dads in the Milk Ad that Tells Me to 'Love What's Real' Consider a Gay Divorce" (p. 23)
"Self-Portrait as the Potato that Flew around My Room" (p. 25)

MAYBE TRANSNESS AND QUEERNESS ARE OUR ONLY HOPES: ON GENDER AND SEXUALITY

My transness and queerness make their way into my writing incessantly because this is the language of my life, the terms by which I make sense of the world around me. Besides, it's fun being trans and queer—I'd highly recommend trying it.

- **EXERCISE**: Write about your body without using any anatomical terms. How would you describe your body and what it does to an alien? How many words can you think of for the shape your body makes on its own and when entangled with others'?

- **DISCUSSION**: Transness and queerness give me hope by reminding me that there are always new ways of existing. What gives you hope? Which parts of the way you live your life create more possibility to be your most joyous self? How do you make space for those ways of living?

REPRESENTATIVE POEMS:

"My Golden Record Melted into Ingots (p. 14)
"Self-Portrait as the Potato that Flew around My Room" (p. 25)

ACKNOWLEDGMENTS

Thank you to Sanjana Bijlani for reminding me that I could always return to the page and for the friendship that makes this poetry possible.

Thank you to everyone who has showed me that poetry is collaboration and community: Kearny Street Workshop and IWL 2020 fellows; Sharon Coleman, my classmates at the Berkeley City College poetry workshops, and fellow editors at *Milvia Street Journal*; Cohort 19, our classmates, faculty, and staff at the Rainier Writing Workshop; and all the trans and queer writers of color alongside whom I write.

Thank you to the students and comrades who fight for, steward, and make small and big magic at the Multicultural Community Center. Thank you to Luna Ramos whose poetry workshop sparked the poem that would become "A Student Asks Me about Empirical Knowledge of the Self as a Prerequisite to Self-Love (and I Fumble the Response)." Thank you Dr. Elisa Diana Huerta, Andrea Preza, Dr. Elizabeth Aranda, and ChE—the models of possibility we shape together make me whole.

Thank you to my families: Pimentel family, Mendoza family, Aspillaga family, my chosen family of loves old and new. Thank you, Nanay, Tatay, and Anthony.

Thank you to everyone whose labor, creativity, empathy, and stubborn insistence make my life possible. I hope that I can make your life even a bit more possible in turn.

Thank you to the folks at Nomadic Press for making this work material.

Poems in this chapbook (sometimes in earlier forms) have appeared in some amazing publications. I am very grateful that some of this work has found homes in the following places:

"On Grammar" in *Cosmonauts Avenue*

"The Takoyaki Vending Machines and I" in *Pine Hills Review*

"I Lean Into the Throat of Summer" and "Self-Portrait as the Potato that Flew around My Room" in *Underblong*

"Nagladlad" in *Apogee*

"Ode to the Moon, the Earth's Only Satellite, with Years of Cognitive Behavioral Therapy" in *Lantern Review*

"The Gay Dads in the Milk Ad that Tells Me to "Love What's Real" Consider a Gay Divorce" in *Peach Mag* (and later anthologized in *Peach Mag's Speculative Mix*)

"Jhené Aiko (The Poet) Reads José Esteban Muñoz and Eats a Pluot in a Bathhouse" in the anthology *LIWANAG 3* published by SOMA Pilipinas and Kearny Street Workshop

antmen pimentel mendoza

antmen pimentel mendoza (he + she) is a Filipinx-American scorpio, bakla, and writer. He was born and raised in South Bay San Diego, California, but is currently based in the East Bay. antmen works at a university cultural center collaborating with students of color on fostering spaces of shared learning, curriculum development, and managing a community-based lending library. She is a student at the Rainier Writing Workshop at Pacific Lutheran University.

4 OTHER WAYS TO SUPPORT NOMADIC PRESS WRITERS

Please consider supporting these funds. You can donate on a one-time or monthly basis from $10–∞ You can also more generally support Nomadic Press by donating to our general fund via nomadicpress. org/donate and by continuing to buy our books.

As always, thank you for your support!

Scan the QR code for more information and/or to donate.

You can also donate at nomadicpress.org/store.

ABOUT THE FUNDS

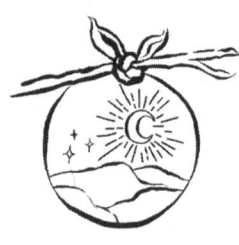

XALAPA FUND

XALAPA FUND

The Xalapa Fund was started in May of 2022 to help offset the airfare costs of Nomadic Press authors to travel to our new retreat space in Xalapa, Veracruz in Mexico. Funds of up to $350 will be dispersed to any Nomadic Press published author who wishes to travel to Xalapa. The funds are kept in a separate bank account and disbursements are overseen by three (3) Nomadic Press authors and Founding Publisher J. K. Fowler.

Inherent in these movements will be cultural exchanges and Nomadic Press will launch a reading series based out of the bookstore/cafe downstairs from the space in August 2022. This series will feature Xalapa-based writers and musicians as well as open-mic slots and will be live streamed to build out relationships between our communities in Oakland, California, Philadelphia, Pennsylvania, and the greater US (and beyond).

EMERGENCY FUND

Right before Labor Day 2020 (and in response to the effects of COVID), Nomadic Press launched its Emergency Fund, a forever fund meant to support Nomadic Press-published writers who have no income, are unemployed, don't qualify for unemployment, have no healthcare, or are just generally in need of covering unexpected or impactful expenses.

Funds are first come, first serve, and are available as long as there is money in the account, and there is a dignity centered internal application that interested folks submit. Disbursements are made for any amount up to $300. All donations made to this fund are kept in a separate account. The Nomadic Press Emergency Fund (NPEF) account and associated processes (like the application) are overseen by Nomadic Press authors and the group meets every month.

BLACK WRITERS FUND

On Juneteenth (June 19) 2020, Nomadic Press launched the Nomadic Press Black Writers Fund (NPBWF), a forever fund that will be directly built into the fabric of our organization for as long as Nomadic Press exists and puts additional monies directly into the pockets of our Black writers at the end of each year.

Here is how it works: $1 of each book sale goes into the fund. At the end of each year, all Nomadic Press authors have the opportunity to voluntarily donate none, part, or all of their royalties to the fund. Anyone from our larger communities can donate to the fund. This is where you come in! At the end of the year, whatever monies are in the fund will be evenly distributed to all Black Nomadic Press authors that have been published by the date of disbursement (mid-to-late December). The fund (and associated, separate bank account) has an oversight team comprised of four authors (Ayodele Nzinga, Daniel B. Summerhill, Dazié Grego-Sykes, and Odelia Younge) + Nomadic Press Executive Director J. K. Fowler.

PAINTING THE STREETS FUND

The Nomadic Press Painting the Streets Fund was launched in February 2022 to support visual arts programs in Oakland flatlands' schools. Its launch coincided with the release of *Painting the Streets: Oakland Uprising in the Time of Rebellion*. Your donations here will go directly into a separate bank account overseen by J. K. Fowler (Nomadic Press), Elena Serrano (Eastside Arts Alliance), Leslie Lopez (EastSide Arts Alliance), Rachel Wolfe-Goldsmith (BAMP), and Andre Jones (BAMP). In addition, all net proceeds from the sale of *Painting the Streets: Oakland Uprising in the Time of Rebellion* will go into this fund. We will share the fund's impact annually on project partner websites. Here are a few schools that we have already earmarked to receive funds: Ile Omode, Madison High School, McClymonds High School, Roosevelt Middle School, Elmhurst Middle School, Castlemont High School, Urban Promise Academy, West Oakland Middle School, and POC Homeschoolers of Oakland.